T0196998

BRINGING

THE

SACRED

TO

LIFE

DHARMA COMMUNICATIONS BOOKS

by John Daido Loori

Bringing the Sacred to Life
The Daily Practice of Zen Ritual

Cave of Tigers
The Living Zen Practice of Dharma Combat

Finding the Still Point
A Beginner's Guide to Zen Meditation

Hearing with the Eye
Photographs from Point Lobos

Invoking Reality
Moral and Ethical Teachings of Zen

Making Love with Light
Contemplating Nature with Words and Photographs

Mountain Record of Zen Talks

Teachings of the Earth
Zen and the Environment

BRINGING
THE
SACRED
TO
LIFE

The Daily Practice of Zen Ritual

JOHN DAIDO LOORI

SHAMBHALA   Boston & London   2008

SHAMBHALA PUBLICATIONS, INC.
Horticultural Hall
300 Massachusetts Avenue
Boston, Massachusetts 02115
www.shambhala.com

Photo credits: page 3: Tate Dogherty; pages 6, 27, 51, 57, 76, 89, 99: Paul
Qaysi; page 13: Brian Lary; pages 18, 37, 65, 68, 79: National Buddhist
Archive; page 30: Robert Aichinger; page 41: Zelenyak Zolatan; page
61: Karen Winton; page 85: M. Ralev; page 102: Dan Colcer.

Printed in the United States of America

⊗This edition is printed on acid-free paper that meets
the American National Standards Institute z39.48 Standard.
♻Shambhala Publications makes every effort to print on recycled
paper. For more information please visit www.shambhala.com.
Distributed in the United States by Penguin Random House LLC
and in Canada by Random House of Canada Ltd

Designed by Lora Zorian

Library of Congress Cataloging-in-Publication Data

Loori, John Daido.
[Celebrating everyday life.]
Bringing the sacred to life: the daily practice of Zen ritual /
John Daido Loori.
p. cm. (Dharma communications books.)
Originally published: Celebrating everyday life. Mt. Tremper, NY:
Zen Home Liturgy, 1999.
ISBN 978-1-59030-533-1 (pbk.: alk. paper)
1. Zen Buddhism—Rituals. 2. Religious life—Zen Buddhism.
I. Title.
BQ9270.2.L67 2008
294.3'438—dc22
2007038238

Contents

MAKING
VISIBLE
THE
INVISIBLE

J UST AS IN the arts of painting, poetry, music, and dance, in Zen liturgy we manifest that which is known to us intuitively in the form of a visible, tangible reality. In this way, liturgy tends to make palpable the common experience of a group. There is, however, very little explanation of liturgy generally available. It is rare to see a substantive work on the subject in Buddhism or any of the other major religions. At best, we're given an explanation of the form, usually with little or no insight as to how the liturgy really functions or what it means. Indeed, liturgy is a very difficult subject to talk about because it is so fundamentally experiential. Talking about it tends to move us further and further from the heart of the matter.

In the religious life of many Americans, liturgy is experienced as little more than a collection of meaningless gestures and rituals. Because it doesn't fit into our scientific reference system, our tendency may be to reject it outright. We seem, in fact, to be a culture with distinctly polarized reactions to liturgy. While at the one end there are those who become very attached to the forms, at the other extreme are those who adamantly reject everything even remotely resembling religious ritual. Yet, in actuality, whether we realize it or not, we are immersed in secular ritual all the time. Liturgy is a constant reaffirmation of the experience of a group of people. From the United States Senate to the Marine Corps to baseball fans enjoying a game at the stadium, there is a liturgical identification between the participants and the events they are involved in.

Ritualistic behavior is an integral part of all life—not only the life of human beings, but every kind of life, from bees, wolves, cats, birds, insects, and worms right down to bacteria. Ritual is simply an inherent aspect of social interaction. Part of the problem we have with liturgy in this country comes about because we like to consider ourselves an essentially

secular culture while, in fact, there is a theistic sup-
position underlying the way most of us understand
how the universe works. This becomes obvious in
how difficult it is for most Americans to recognize
sacred ritual or liturgy that does not address a divine
being. Put most simply, the question we have to deal
with in nontheistic Zen liturgy is, "What is the ritual
about if the Buddha is not a god?" In Zen the question of a divine being is not central and, instead, the
emphasis is on the ground of being, the Buddha nature, which is not separate from the nature of the self.

All of Zen's rites and rituals are constantly
pointing to the same place, to the realization of no
separation between the self and the ten thousand
things. Zen liturgy is *upaya,* skillful means. Like zazen
and all the other areas of training, it functions as
a way of uncovering the truth which is the life of
each one of us. Zen study, face-to-face teaching, work
practice, academic study, art practice, body practice,
the Precepts all point to the same place: the nature of
the self. Skillful means are necessary because each one
of us, just as we are, is already perfect and complete.
We lack nothing. What we seek is exactly where we
stand. But knowing this doesn't do anything; it is not
a matter of knowing. It has to be realized as the functioning of our lives. And for practice to function, for
liturgy to function, it must first be wholeheartedly

engaged. Practice is always with the whole body and mind. Just imitating the honchos, aping the form—"monkey see, monkey do"—is a dead end. It is like binding oneself without a rope.

The first morning service at the monastery each day is dedicated to Shakyamuni Buddha and expresses our identification with him. Shakyamuni Buddha is not dead—a hall full of buddhas identifies with him. But what does "Buddha" mean? What does "enlightenment" mean? Is enlightenment something that you get or that is given to you? Of course not. This is why we say that there are no Zen teachers and there is nothing to teach, pointing again to the fact that we already have what we seek. This first daily service expresses that wisdom. It is an identification with what we already have—our Buddha nature, the intrinsic enlightenment of each one of us.

The service is also an expression of gratitude for the teachings of the historic Buddha, for the fact that after he realized himself, he didn't just take off for some mountaintop retreat with the attitude, "Well, I got what I was seeking for the last eight years—to hell with everybody else!" Instead, he stayed in the world for forty-seven years, teaching the unteachable, so that this incredible Dharma could be transmitted mind-to-mind through successive generations from India to China to Japan, and now to America.

Expressing gratitude is transformative, just as transformative as expressing complaint. Imagine an experiment involving two people. One is asked to spend ten minutes each morning and evening expressing gratitude (there is always something to be grateful for), while the other is asked to spend the same amount of time practicing complaining (there is, after all, always something to complain about). One of the subjects is saying things like, "I hate my job. I can't stand this apartment. Why can't I make enough money? My spouse doesn't get along with me. That dog next door never stops barking and I just can't stand this neighborhood." The other is saying things like, "I'm really grateful for the opportunity to work; there are so many people these days who can't even find a job. And I'm sure grateful for my health. What a gorgeous day; I really like this fall breeze." They do this experiment for a year. Guaranteed, at the end of that year the person practicing complaining will have deeply reaffirmed all his negative "stuff" rather than having let it go, while the one practicing gratitude will be a very grateful person. What you practice is what you are; practice and the goal of practice are identical, cause and effect are one reality. Expressing gratitude can, indeed, change our way of seeing ourselves and the world.

The second morning service is dedicated to the lineage of teachers. We chant the names of the Indian, Chinese, and Japanese *Daioshos* ("Great Teachers") from Shakyamuni Buddha down to the present time and place, and express our gratitude to them, because without their dedication to transmitting the Dharma mind-to-mind, this practice would not have survived. What has survived in our liturgy is the Buddhadharma itself, beyond all the ideas and the words that might describe it. The Buddhadharma can only go from human to human, from buddha to buddha, from mind to mind. That is why it remains so alive, so vibrant; and that is how it will flow to future generations. It takes on the shape of the container that holds it, adapting itself to time, place, and condition.

If we were practicing "by the book"—by the words and ideas that describe reality rather than by reality itself—Zen training would not have lasted very long, especially in this country. Going by the book would have us practicing something designed 2,500 years ago in an entirely different culture. The historic Buddha didn't have to deal with our kinds of questions. He had never heard of nuclear bombs or ecological destruction, and because most of his students were monks, there were very few questions about marital and sexual relationships, or about rais-

ing children. If the teaching does not take the shape
of the vessel that contains it, it is dead teaching.

Books contain dead teaching. Live teaching
comes from living people and who then transmit it to
living people. The truth has not changed, the basic
questions have not changed, the basic problem has
not changed. What has changed is the skillful means
by which we come to realize ourselves. In this second
morning service we recognize the effort and flexibility of the teachers who have kept the Dharma alive as
it made its way here.

The third morning service is dedicated to our
family heritage, our personal ancestors. To be asked
to bow to our parents is a major stumbling block for
many American students. "I can't bow to my parents," we say, "I hate them!" The fact is that until we
can accept our parents, we can't really accept ourselves. If you haven't made peace with your parents,
no matter who or what they are or how they dis-
appointed your expectations, then you can have no
real peace with yourself. This identifying with one's
own genetic lineage, one's parents and their parents back through successive generations, is an important Buddhist practice. We begin to see how at
this time and place the two streams of life come together, the genetic transmission of our family heritage

and the mind-to-mind transmission of the Buddha. They come alive in the life of each one of us.

The fourth morning service is a healing service for those who are gravely ill or in need of our support. In the dedication to the service, one of the lines reads, "Whenever this devoted invocation is sent forth, it is perceived and subtly answered." But who is it that is being invoked? Who is the subtle answerer? Each one of us and the ten thousand things are interdependent, interpenetrating in time and in space. Where are the perceiver and respondent to be found? All of the sutras we chant and all of the dedications that are recited by the chant leader are chock-full of koans; and like all koans, they remain dark to the mind but radiant to the heart. As our practice deepens and our understanding develops, we open more and more to the teaching, and the truth of liturgy reveals itself to us.

In addition to the daily morning services, there are other formal liturgies used at the monastery, such as the gathas recited before meals and work. These liturgies precede activities that we don't often engage consciously, and provide a transition, a moment of focus to stop and reflect on what we're doing. Every time we receive a meal we consume life; we kill living things in order to sustain our own life. Buddhism does not differentiate between higher and lower life forms—a cabbage is every bit as holy as a cow. Life is life, and we must consume it in order to live. Only when we do this with full awareness can we take complete responsibility for our action. Hence, there is reflection and thanksgiving before a meal.

Liturgy also addresses and informs the moments of important transitions in our lives—birth, marriage, ordination, death—as opportunities for us to reflect on the teaching and to see how it applies to what we're doing. At a funeral ceremony, for example, a poem is addressed to the dead person. Where is the dead person? How could he or she hear it? Who is hearing it? What is it that is born? What is it that dies? Buddhism teaches that life is the unborn and death the unextinguished. What is life? Do you understand?

In the case of marriage, the couple is already united in their own minds, but their union is invisible to others until it is revealed and manifested in the marriage ceremony. A formal Zen marriage ceremony is performed only after the couple have already married one another—only they can marry themselves. It is the same with ordination of monks. The public ceremony isn't done until, by virtue of the student's personal commitment and vows, he or she has already become a monk. The ceremony merely makes it visible to the community so that everyone can then share and participate in the event. There is no magic to be given; the magic is already theirs—and yours. All liturgy can do is render it visible to those who love the monk or the couple who have married. This making visible the invisible is at the heart of the matter.

What does it mean to make visible something which is invisible? Essentially, it means to bring that something into the awareness of the six consciousnesses. Buddhist teaching recognizes six areas of conscious awareness, rather than the five we're familiar with from Western physiology and psychology. In addition to the five organs of perception—eye, ear, nose, tongue, and body (or seeing, hearing, smelling, tasting, and touching)—Buddhism identifies mind itself as an "organ" that perceives. The organ of perception and the object it perceives, together with consciousness, produce what we call reality. So, a thing becomes real (what we call "real") when the organ of perception, its object, and consciousness come together. My eye, the object that it sees, and consciousness combine to form a tangible reality. When you consider mind as one of the organs of perception, the concept of reality expands beyond the boundaries usually accepted in the West. The object of mind is thought; mind, thought, and consciousness thus create a reality. The thought of hitting someone is just as much an action

as physically hitting, or expressing the desire to hit, someone. And just as speech and action produce karma, so do our thoughts.

"Making visible" means that we are able to perceive, through these organs of perception, that something is there, though invisible. What is it that is invisible? What is the common experience of the Buddhist community that is restated in our liturgy? What is it that we recreate through the practice of Zen liturgy?

Another way of seeing liturgy is as an expression of mutual identity. In bringing our hands together in *gassho*, we take an idea and turn it into action. When you make something an action it becomes clarified and concrete. We gassho before entering the zendo, before accepting food, and as we greet one another; with each gassho we identify with the place, the object, the person. We acknowledge in our action the fact that all the dualities come together to create one reality.

This identification is why Zen services are not considered worship. Worship requires that there be something which is bigger, higher, or beyond ourselves. In a Zen service we identify with the Buddha— we practice the fact that Buddha and I are the same thing, that you and I are the same thing. The teaching in Zen liturgy always comes from the point of view of realization. Nothing is explained. It proceeds as if everyone knew. One buddha speaks to another buddha. To hear what is being said we have to shift our way of hearing and abandon our reference system. It has to be seen directly and immediately.

Because of this directness, immediacy, and intimacy, Zen liturgy functions as an empowerment of the self. Suddenly you realize that it all boils down to you, that you are responsible for the entire universe, the whole catastrophe. When no-separation is realized, you can no longer blame, you can no longer be a victim; there is only the master. And that empowerment comes from yourself to yourself. With the wisdom of realization, compassion necessarily arises. Compassion is the actualization of wisdom in the activity of the world. When the self is forgotten, only the ten thousand things remain. Everything is realized as nothing but yourself. Compassion, then, is nothing but taking good care of yourself. If someone falls, you pick them up; if the environment is polluted, you clean it up. The whole world is you. Intimately and personally taking good care of it is compassion.

Unfortunately, most of us try to understand the intimate experience of liturgy in the same way we understand science or how to drive a car. When that kind of analysis is applied to liturgy, it kills liturgy. Liturgy becomes nothing more than the inane babbling of people imitating something they neither realize nor are working to realize. Analysis doesn't reveal what is happening in liturgy. It doesn't free us; instead, it paralyzes us.

Unquestionably, liturgy requires a degree of faith. This whole practice requires faith. From the beginning, a certain amount of faith is necessary because, initially, nothing that we're doing has been verified by our own experience. We practice faith all the time in contexts we don't think of as religious or particularly liturgical. When you lay a ten dollar bill on top of the counter while waiting for your bag of groceries, there is a period of time when you have neither your money nor your groceries, only trust. You get on a bus and pay the fare before you've gotten a ride, trusting that the driver and the bus company will get you where you want to go. We trust our doctors, our lawyers, and our dentists. We trust our partners and our mates. The world works on trust, agreement, and commitment.

The trust that operates in Zen practice, however, is based on faith in yourself, on a feeling you have now, not on something you expect to gain or believe you will receive from others. It is not, "If I have faith, something good will happen." We practice zazen in the faith that we *can* realize ourselves, but, ultimately, we *must* realize ourselves. It is the same with Zen liturgy. It begins with an act of faith, but as our practice progresses and develops, our understanding of it changes.

In thirteenth-century Japan, when Master Dogen began teaching at Eiheiji Monastery, he found that the practice of liturgy had largely become a meaningless imitation of form. In a radical step to revitalize the training, he taught his monks a new kind of liturgy. He used the everyday activities of life as sacred liturgy. This is ultimately what Zen practice is about: descending the mountain, manifesting that which has been realized in everything that we do. Zen practice is not an activity that takes place in the world but, rather, the activity of the world itself.

We live in a time and place of incredible moral and ethical disintegration—in politics, government, business, and in religion itself. It is interesting to look at what is going on in this country and question what is behind the problems we are experiencing. We continue to reelect to political positions people who have been clearly shown guilty of violations of the public trust. It seems insane that this is happening. Some of the most vociferous and well-publicized religious leaders, not only in the right wing of religion but in the left as well, not only in Western religions but the Eastern ones, break their own vows,

their own rules. In the business world, corruption and deceit seem to be at an all-time high, from individuals cheating a little bit on their income taxes to insider trading on Wall Street. Suppliers of services rip off their customers; contractors add a little extra sand to the concrete to save on costs. Why does all this happen?

When you really look at it, you begin to understand that corruption is about power—worldly power, not spiritual power. Worldly power has to do with money or position, the ability to control or manipulate people or things. Spiritual power, on the other hand, has to do with realizing yourself. When you realize yourself, the opposite of manipulation happens. Not that people with spiritual power burn money; they don't—that would be stupid. They just don't use it to manipulate and control other people. When no-self is realized, other is realized as nothing but the self. That is what it means to be enlightened by the ten thousand things.

Even within religions, that spiritual power hasn't generally become manifest in the personal lives of the people involved. Somehow the teachings that have to do with the spiritual power of religion, whatever religion a person may profess, are rarely engaged to the stage where they are actualized in everyday affairs. For me, the key to this actualization is liturgy. In our liturgy, expressing it in our gestures, voice, and thought, we renew, confirm, and restate our Buddha nature. We embody the life of a buddha.

To confirm and renew means that wherever you are and whatever your life is, the teachings will manifest. If you are a lawyer, the teachings will manifest in your law practice. If you are a nurse, they will manifest in your nursing. If you are a householder with children, they will manifest in how you raise your kids. And if you are a business person, the teachings will manifest in your business practices. That is the way the teachings of the Buddha are going to reach out into our society. There is a lot of talk about Buddhism in the West, but few serious, committed practitioners. Still, that handful is enough if practice continues. When we practice, life is made easier, not more difficult. Practice doesn't bind us; it makes us free. Greed, anger, and ignorance bind us. The teachings free us; or, to put it more accurately, they help us to realize the inherent freedom that is already there and that has been there from the very beginning.

Somehow, we are able to confuse reality and the make-believe worlds we create. And much of what we create is based on what we have been told as we were growing up. We are each conditioned by our culture, parents, teachers, and peers, and then we proceed to live our entire life out of that conditioning.

That conditioning defines who we think we are. All of these authoritative people have told us who we are, so we go on to manifest their predictions. This practice, every bit of it, is about going beyond all of that conditioning, finding out for ourselves who we are, and then living our life in accordance with what we have realized. That is what freedom is about.

In America we usually have a negative reaction to "observing reflection and gratitude." We tend to rebel against the teachings and try to change them to suit our own particular perceptions of what we think they should be, stripping the teachings of their richness by eliminating an important part of the upaya, carefully evolved over centuries of practice. At the other extreme, there are also people who, under the guise of Zen practice, blindly imitate the sounds and forms of the training. This is definitely not what Zen is about. Great faith, great doubt, great determination (the three pillars of real practice) keep that rote imitation from happening. Great doubt, working in dynamic tension with great faith, along with the deep commitment to continue, keep the student's active edge alive. Zen training is neither rebelling nor conforming. What is it then?

All of this upaya, all of the teaching, every aspect of the liturgy, is a secret. It is the secret to world peace, being revealed in the eighty-four thousand subtle gestures that comprise our practice. It is the secret to social transformation, ecological harmony, marriage and relationships; the secret to raising children, dancing, chopping wood and carrying water. The secret is this incredible Dharma dance called life. But it must be danced to be realized. It is not the words that describe it. It is not the ideas we have about it. It is the thing itself. The dance, the bow, the voice. This is not an empty exhibition of form. It is the actualization of the buddhas and ancestors of the past, present, and future.

INVOKING

OUR

LIVES

PEOPLE ENTERING ZEN PRACTICE have many inquiries about liturgy. One of the frequently asked questions has to do with *dharanis*. Because dharanis are not chanted in English, people often assume they are Japanese. But the dharanis we chant are mostly just sounds. There are dharanis which are used by officiants in certain liturgies and some dharanis which are transmitted as part of the oral teachings at the end of formal training.

The obvious questions that follow are: "What does chanting sounds have to do with the Dharma? What does this have to do with me and my life?" In order to appreciate the function of sound and its relationship to consciousness, we need to see how certain sounds create a particular state of consciousness. The best way to understand this is to recall that when you are in pain and your whole body is aching, to simply groan—oooh—feels good. Making that sound releases the tension and relieves the pain. Similarly, when you are feeling great, you want to shout with joy—yippee! The shout expresses the feeling that has built up inside you. A dharani is composed of sounds and those sounds create a state of consciousness. It is like the seed syllable Om, which creates a state of mind that is very quiet, still, and expansive.

Another question intimately pertaining to liturgy concerns the effect of thoughts on the creation of karma. If what you manifest with your body creates karma, and how you express yourself in words creates karma, what you do with your mind also creates karma. How does this happen? Whether we realize it or not we are constantly communicating with others and the whole universe with our thoughts. If you have a big smile on your face but hate someone's guts, the message of hate will still get across. Most of the time we are very preoccupied and our minds are busy, so we don't pick up on a conscious level what someone may be actually communicating with their thoughts, be it fear, anger, or resentment.

Children tend to be very conscious of these underlying thoughts. The younger we are, the more intuitive we are. Animals also have this uncanny ability to "read" others accurately. I don't know what the scientific explanation for this communication of thoughts is, but the reality of my experience is that we are always communicating on this level.

There is not only formal religious liturgy. There is the communal liturgy of a football game—when the band plays, the players all run onto the field, and the crowd gets whipped up into a frenzy. That is a liturgy that creates a particular kind of consciousness—football liturgy. So it is with baseball and with the Supreme Court. Almost everything we do collectively contains a ritual which expresses the common experience of the group.

In Christianity, for example, the religious experiences have to do with God, Jesus, the soul, and heaven. Churches and cathedrals are designed to communicate these notions; they are vast, beautiful, extending upward. Christian chanting reflects this otherworldliness. Gregorian chants lift you out of yourself into heaven. Buddhist chants, on the other hand, particularly in Zen, tend to be very grounded, driven by a steady rhythm, like a heartbeat, very much in the here-and-now. Zen altars strive for a similar effect of simplicity and directness. The sounds and forms of Zen liturgy are a direct expression of an appreciation of the nature of reality arising in Zen practice.

When a monk asked Zen Master Ch'ang-sha about dharanis, Ch'ang-sha didn't go into a long explanation. He simply pointed to the left of his meditation seat and said, "This monk is reciting a dharani." The monk continued, "Is there anyone else who can recite it?" Ch'ang-sha pointed to the right of his meditation seat and said, "That monk is reciting it too." The monk asked, "Then why can't I hear it?" Ch'ang-sha said, "This is its great virtue. How can it not be seen and heard?" This answer doesn't seem to make sense. The monk cannot hear it but how can it not be seen or heard? Ch'ang-sha continued. "It's real chanting that makes no sound and in really listening to it, there is no hearing." The monk completely missed this point and asked, "Doesn't sound enter into the nature of the Dharma realms?" Ch'ang-sha clarified his point further. He said, "Leaving form to observe form isn't a correct view. Leaving sound seeking to listen is a debased hearing." In other words, to separate yourself from sound in order to hear it is not what liturgy is about. It is about intimacy. Intimacy goes beyond sight and sound.

In ceremony there are forms and there are sounds; there is understanding, and there is believing.

In liturgy there is only intimacy. Intimacy means no gaps, no separation, not two. Intimate understanding is not like ordinary understanding. Ordinary understanding is seeing with the eye and hearing with the ear; intimacy is seeing with the ear and hearing with the eye. How do you see with the ear and hear with the eye? Let go of the eye, and the whole body-and-mind is nothing but the eye; let go of the ear, and the whole universe is nothing but the ear. You will never grasp this by seeing it dualistically, by seeing yourself and "it" as two separate things.

Bodhidharma said that invocation is not about chanting words or sounds. You invoke with the mind. You do liturgy with the mind. You do zazen with the mind. When you enter the mind of zazen you enter a sacred space. It doesn't matter whether you are sitting on top of a mountain, in a zendo, or at the intersection of 42nd Street and Broadway. It doesn't matter what activity you are doing. The mind of zazen always opens a sacred space. It is in that sacred space that the dharani and the Dharma exist. That is the meaning of the passage: Let go of the eye, and the whole body-and-mind is nothing but the eye; let go of the ear, and the whole universe is nothing but the ear.

Awareness is much more than the functioning of a single organ of perception, and is even beyond all the organs of perception added together. There is a group of blind people who are studying karate and it is pretty remarkable. These students are totally blind, but they are able to sense a person coming toward them and to respond with an appropriate karate move. Another example of this awareness was shown to me in a film about a group of blind people who climbed Mt. Kilimanjaro. At one point during the expedition, all the group's flashlight batteries ran down and people were caught in the dark. All the porters and trip leaders with sight made a big deal out of the problem and the blind people had to take over and keep the group going. In true perception, all the senses converge: eye, ear, nose, tongue, body, and mind. They are one reality and that reality fills the universe.

In our Buddha hall there are three figures on the altar. In the middle sits the Buddha. On one side is Manjushri Bodhisattva. He rides a lion and carries a sword. It is a double-edged sword. One side kills the ego and the other side gives life. Manjushri is the Bodhisattva of Wisdom. In other words, Manjushri has a clear eye of wisdom. That is why Manjushri is always covering his eyes. Avalokiteshvara, also called Kannon or Kuan Yin, sits on the other side. Usually depicted in the female form, she is the Goddess of Compassion. What the word Avalokiteshvara literally means is "the hearer of the cries of the world." The

Bodhisattva of Compassion responds to the needs of people through sound. When there is a cry for help, she responds. She takes the form that is appropriate to the situation.

Avalokiteshvara is always covering her ears. In intimacy there is no separation; in complete hearing, there is no separation. The kind of hearing that Avalokiteshvara does is the hearing of whole body-and-mind intimacy. No gaps. The kind of seeing Manjushri does is whole body-and-mind seeing. No gaps.

We are the first generation of American practitioners. We are involved in a very important process: the coming of Buddhism to the West, manifesting in a western form. Buddhism was in India and China and other Asian countries for hundreds of years. When it first came to Asia it was very fresh, vibrant, and vital. That is the way it is here in the West right now—very exciting. In fact our Dharma brothers and sisters in Japan, China, Korea, and Vietnam look at us and the way we practice here with awe and envy. They admire the way that both monastics and lay students practice with the same vigor that was prevalent in the Golden Age of Zen. But after an initial period of vitality, Buddhism declined in Asian countries, losing its original spirit in popularization, dilution, and rote repetition.

That is why it is really important for us to appreciate what is going on in the different areas of our training. Otherwise practice is going to decline here as well. We can't take it for granted. When I was quite young and studied religion with Jesuits and nuns, I was truly interested in how they were seeing the nature of the universe, how they understood it, and how they manifested their understanding. I believed everything I was told and did the practices I was taught with my whole heart. But I began to notice that everybody didn't take it seriously. The priest didn't take things seriously. He would be talking a mile a minute as he walked past a church, then make the sign of the cross in the midst of his conversation without dropping a word. It was only a reflex action. It didn't mean anything. It wasn't done with the whole body-and-mind. It wasn't even conscious. It was no different than scratching his head.

The danger of irrelevance is always lurking in our inattention. Buddhism in this country can easily go the route of empty forms if we are not dedicated to making every moment of our lives count. At the monastery, we are involved in liturgy every morning, noon, and night. These practices are repetitious and it is easy to lose touch with whole body-and-mind intimacy. If there is no whole body-and-mind intimacy, there is no zazen, no liturgy, no *dokusan*, no work practice, no art practice, no body practice. All we have without whole body-and-mind intimacy is the form, and that is not worth a thing when it comes to living your life. Please don't take this practice lightly. Know that in every single aspect of it there are multiple levels of depth to be seen, appreciated, realized, and actualized. It is only then that we give life to the Buddha.

METAPHYSICS
OF
COOKING

ALL OF MASTER DOGEN'S teachings point to how our everyday lives are the very ground of our Zen practice. Whether he was writing a poem, giving instructions on how to clean one's teeth, cook a meal, or do a job—he was always revealing the sixteen-foot golden body of the Buddha, the teachings of the Tathagata. It is exceedingly odd that so many of us are puzzled when it comes to realizing our Zen practice in daily living situations. "How can I practice in my life?" students repeatedly ask. This practice is about your life; that is all it is about.

Master Dogen made the position of chief cook, *tenzo*, key in his monastery, usually second in importance only to the abbot. Chief cook is much more than a "hash-slinger." In fact, the cook has enormous responsibility and opportunity to teach. In traditional Japanese Zen monasteries, an older, mature Roshi serves as tenzo. He or she may have many assistants, but the Roshi provides the leadership and teaching.

The teaching entitled "Instructions to the Chief Cook" appears in the *Eihei Shingi*, the monastic regulations. Some of Dogen's most profound teachings can be found in these rules of the monastery.

> Take up a green vegetable leaf and turn it into a sixteen-foot golden body; take the sixteen-foot golden body and turn it into a green vegetable leaf. This is the miraculous transformation—a work of Buddha that benefits all sentient beings.

Because our *sangha* at this monastery is still young and maturing, the position of tenzo is assigned to one of the senior monks, with the cook working as an assistant. It is the tenzo's responsibility to supervise and train the succession of cooks who pass through here, and to do that in accord with the spirit of Master Dogen. Each time a new cook comes to dokusan, I ask them if they can take up a green vegetable leaf and turn it into a sixteen-foot golden body, or take a sixteen-foot golden body and turn it into a green vegetable leaf. It becomes a koan they work with for as long as they are the cook.

What does it mean to take up the green vegetable leaf and turn it into a sixteen-foot golden body? The sixteen-foot golden body is the body of the Buddha, the golden body of the Tathagata, the golden body of suchness.

It includes the heavens and encompasses the earth; it transcends both sacred and mundane. On the tips of a hundred thousand weeds, the marvelous mind of nirvana.

Weeds are images for defilement and delusion. So, on the tips of hundreds of thousands of weeds, of delusions, can be found the marvelous mind of nirvana. It is the marvelous mind of nirvana that was transmitted by the Buddha to Mahakashyapa on Vulture Peak, 2,500 years ago.

At that time, the Buddha took up a flower and came out to address an assembly of thousands. He held up the flower and twirled it. Only Mahakashyapa smiled and blinked his eyes. The Buddha said, "I have the marvelous mind of nirvana, the exquisite teaching of formless form. I now hand it over to

Mahakashyapa." What was the Buddha's intent? What is it that Mahakashyapa saw that no one else saw? What is it that was transmitted, and what is it that was received? Master Dogen takes up the green vegetable leaf in the same way as Buddha took up the flower.

In Zen, we say that there is nothing to transmit and nothing to receive. And yet, somehow, Buddha singled out Mahakashyapa as the only one in the assembly who understood what he was teaching. If you say that the Dharma cannot be transmitted, then why did Buddha say that he "now gives it to Mahakashyapa?" Was he ripping off all the other people there? What if everyone had smiled and blinked their eyes—would he have transmitted to two thousand people? On the other hand, what if nobody had smiled and blinked their eyes—would the Dharma have just disappeared from the face of the earth?

You should understand the essential matter of this holding up of the flower and the smile of Mahakashyapa. If you can understand that, you can understand what Master Dogen is asking here. You will understand the line, "On the tips of a hundred thousand weeds, the marvelous mind of nirvana." You will understand how it transcends both the sacred and the mundane.

From deep within the forest of brambles, the one bright pearl illuminates the ten thousand things. The forest of brambles is the forest of barriers, of difficulties, of pain and suffering, delusion and ignorance; it is samsara itself. And from deep within that forest of brambles, one bright pearl illuminates the ten thouand things; its radiance touches everything, sacred and mundane, heaven and earth alike.

The point that is being made with, "Take up the green vegetable leaf and turn it into a sixteen-foot golden body" appears many times in the literature, though different devices are used. In one of the koans, Manjushri asks Sudana to bring him something that is not medicine. Sudana searches and searches. He finally comes back to Manjushri and says, "I cannot find anything that is not medicine." Manjushri replies, "Then bring me something that is medicine." And Sudana bends down, plucks a blade of grass and hands it to him. Manjushri holds up the blade of grass and says, "This has the power to kill and to give life." And so it is with the green vegetable leaf.

Buddha asked Manjushri to build him a temple. Manjushri plucked a blade of grass, touched it to the ground, and said, "Here is your temple." The Buddha approved. All of it is the miraculous transformation of a Buddha that benefits all sentient beings. How? How does it benefit all sentient beings?

It is easy to intellectualize what Dogen and Man-jushri say. That is the nest; the nest of understanding. Master Uchiyama comments on this in his book *From the Zen Kitchen to Enlightenment*, saying,

> Even when handling just one leaf of green, do so in such a way that the leaf manifests the fullness of its potential, which in turn allows the illumination of Buddha to radi-ate through it. This is the power of func-tioning whose nature is incapable of being grasped with the rational mind, and one which operates without hindrance in a most natural way. At the same time, this power operates in our lives to clarify and settle activities beneficial to all living things.

If you understand Dogen's metaphysics of cook-ing, you understand the Buddha's metaphysics of life. It is not about isolating oneself; it is about living in the world, about cooking a meal, eating a meal, cleaning the teeth, using the lavatory, raising a child, driving a car, doing a job, having a relationship. In other words, it is all of the ten thousand things that take place from morning until evening each day of our life. Yet somehow we struggle through those ordinary everyday activities. It is not so settled; as

Master Uchiyama says, "It is not so clear; it is not so beneficial to either self or other." The reason for that is separation—the illusion of separateness, the illusion of a self that is separate and distinct from the rest of the universe, the illusion of a self that is separate and distinct from the green vegetable leaf, from the marvelous mind of nirvana, from the sixteen-foot golden body of the Buddha, from your lover, from your parents, from your children, from the people of Africa and Bosnia, from this great earth itself. They are not one and one and one and one; they are not separate. It is just one great pearl.

We should realize that one great pearl manifests constantly in the myriad activities that surround us. It exists in a speck of dust; it exists in vast space. That is the "It" that includes heaven and encompasses the earth; that is the "It" that transcends both the sacred and mundane and appears on the tips of the hundred thousand grasses and weeds. Dogen is speaking about intimacy—whole body and mind intimacy. But when we think of intimacy we think of some kind of unity that blinds and deafens us, that renders us nonexistent. The Buddha Way is beyond being and non-being, beyond existence and nonexistence, beyond the sacred and the mundane. It doesn't fall onto either side.

We think of, "No eye, ear, nose, tongue, body,

mind" as intimacy, but that is only one side. The other side is "eye, ear, nose, tongue, body, mind." These two sides are two aspects of the truth, two aspects of "It." What is that? What is it that is neither form nor emptiness, neither sacred nor mundane, neither heaven nor hell, self nor other, being nor nonbeing?

The intimacy that Master Dogen speaks of is whole body and mind intimacy. He talks of it again and again throughout his work. "Seeing form with the whole body and mind, hearing sound with the whole body and mind, one understands it intimately."

Take the sixteen-foot golden body and turn it into a green vegetable leaf. This is a miracle, transforming a green vegetable leaf into the sixteen-foot golden body of thusness. Thusness is "this-very-momentness." There is no before, there is no after. This moment contains a hundred thousand eons. It is past; it is present; it is future—all at once. And it arrives as it leaves, simultaneously.

This is the miraculous transformation—a work of the Buddha that benefits all sentient beings. This includes you yourself. Do you understand? Do you understand that he is not speaking of eminent masters of the past? He is not speaking of buddhas and ancestors, of Maitreya Buddha of the future. He is describing you and your life with all the blemishes showing as the marvelous mind of nirvana.

It is wonderful to bring yourself to the present moment. But that is not what we are talking about here; we are talking about more than that. We are talking about the present moment filling the universe, reaching everywhere, swallowing this great earth itself so that there is no place to stand, no place to put this gigantic body. Dogen says to the chief cook,

> Do not see with ordinary eyes, and do not think with ordinary mind. Take up a blade of grass and construct a Treasure King's land. Enter into a particle of dust and turn the great Dharma wheel. Do not arouse disdainful mind when you prepare a broth of wild grasses; do not arouse joyful mind when you prepare a fine cream soup. Where there is no disdain, how can there be distaste? Thus do not be careless even when you work with poor materials, and sustain your efforts even when you have excellent materials. Never change your attitude according to the materials.

In other words, always have the utmost respect.

We can say the same thing about all sentient beings. When you are talking to a beggar in the street, or talking to the President of the United States, it should be in the same way, with the same respect. But that is not what happens. We wet our pants when we are talking to the president and we look down our noses when we are talking to the beggar in the street.

"Never change your attitude according to your materials. If you do, it is like varying your truth when speaking with different people—then you are not a true practitioner of the Way." Whether it is a child, someone lying on their deathbed, a peer, a superior, or a junior—each and every one deserves the same respect. If it can start there, it can go to the ten thousand things: every tree, every blade of grass, every animal, every adversary—not two. If you can see it that way, you can understand the essential principle of this incredible Dharma, the essential teaching of the great Diamond Net of Indra, where everything interpenetrates with everything else, everything is mutually causal. We share the same causality. What you do and what happens to you are the same thing. Master Dogen says, "This is the way to turn things while being turned by things."

In another fascicle he states, "To advance the self and to realize the ten thousand things is not the true Dharma; to realize that the ten thousand things advance and realize the self is the true teaching." To turn the ten thousand things, and to be turned by the ten thousand things—this is the interpenetration of differences. And you can only do that when you really trust yourself; you can only do that when you truly understand that self and other are two parts of the same reality. Just as form is exactly emptiness and emptiness is exactly form, so too is self exactly other and other exactly self.

That is why you have to see, sooner or later, that it all comes down to you. The whole catastrophe depends on you, however it manifests. Whether it manifests as joy or whether it manifests as pain and suffering, it all comes home to you. What you do and what happens to you are the same thing. Realize that fully and there is no way you can avoid taking responsibility. And when you take responsibility, you empower yourself; you bring freedom home. You can no longer blame. You can no longer say, "He made me angry," because only you can make you angry. When you realize that completely you empower yourself to do something about anger. You may say that "I am tense, and my life is full of stress because of my lousy job." But when you realize that the cause of stress and the effect of stress are the same thing, your way of working with it becomes very different. When you realize responsibility, you realize that sickness and medicine heal each other.

What we search for is everywhere—on the tips of a hundred thousand weeds, in the voice of a child, the growl of an adversary, the barriers we encounter in the workplace, the pain and suffering that we heap upon each other, the peace and joy that we try to create. All of it is samsara; all of it is nirvana. Samsara is precisely nirvana, nirvana is precisely samsara; they are not two separate things.

How can we doubt this incredible teaching of Dogen that takes us into the kitchen, and says, "Look! Chopping these carrots is a manifestation of the Way of the Buddha, cooking this cabbage leaf is a manifestation of the Way of the Buddha."

There is a man who serves as cook when we do *sesshins* in New Zealand who embodies this teaching beautifully. He learned his trade from his father, and then became a cook in the New Zealand Air Force, and somehow ended up in Nelson, New Zealand, where we do our retreats. He makes the best vegetarian cooking I have ever had in my life. It is really beautiful and important how he cooks, the way he handles actual cabbage leaves during a caretaking period. He scalds cabbage leaves in boiling water. He puts one in, and takes it out, and feels it, and puts it in, and takes it out. He handles that cabbage leaf as if it were his child; he handles it with loving-kindness, with intimacy, with joy, and with profound respect. It makes all the difference in the world how that food is prepared, how it tastes, and the way it affects all of us. That is why the chief cook is one of the most important officers of a monastery. To nourish people is not just a matter of putting food in their belly; it is the nourishment of the whole body and mind. If there is anger and confusion in the preparation of the food, people eat anger and confusion; if there is wisdom, compassion, and love, we eat wisdom, compassion, and love. Life nourishes us, we in turn nourish each other, and return our lives to the ten thousand things.

METAPHYSICS
OF
EATING

MASTER DOGEN TAUGHT: "The practice of eating is the essential truth of all dharmas. At the very moment of eating we merge with ultimate reality. Thus Dharma is eating and eating is Dharma, and this eating is full of holy joy and ecstasy."

Master Dogen has a marvelous way of bringing the Dharma alive, and using everyday affairs as the platform of his teachings. He took the most mundane activities and transformed them into gems of spiritual training.

Oryoki, one of the practices he established, is the monastic ceremonial meal taken during a silent retreat or sesshin. It's a very precise and conscious way of eating. And it is probably the most elaborate ceremony that we do. It starts off with a series of drum rolls that have the whole building thundering, as the cook and the head monk bring in the food offering to the Buddha. We begin by giving and receiving. In that process of giving and receiving, there is equality and unity. We receive the teachings, we give our gratitude. We receive the food from the ten thousand things, we offer the food back to the ten thousand things as our life and practice. And in that giving and receiving is the perfect harmony—the wisdom of the other shore.

After ceremonially opening the nested bowls and laying out the utensils, each person is served by the servers. With the opportunity to serve comes an appreciation for being able to do that, being able to support others' practice. The same feeling arises in the kitchen for the cook in preparing the meal that will nourish the life of all beings.

When served, each person takes just the right amount. Just the right amount is different for every individual. It is the amount that is necessary to sustain life and practice. Yasutani Roshi used to say that you should stop eating before you are full: that's just the right amount. And each person has to determine that for themselves.

As the ceremony unfolds we begin to see that we are dealing with eating as a celebration of the Dharma, as the joyful occasion of thanksgiving. Since we took just the right amount, every single morsel is consumed, every grain of rice is taken up and eaten. After we have cleared all the food from the bowls, we then use a spatula to scrape up any remaining food and eat it. The hot water is brought in and poured into the first bowl, and that bowl is cleaned with the spatula. The water is then transferred to the second bowl and the first bowl is dried. The utensils are cleaned in the second bowl, dried, and put away. The second bowl is cleaned and the water is poured into the third bowl. The second bowl is dried and nested in the first. The third bowl is cleaned and the waste water is drunk. No traces remain. Every bit of food, including the waste water, is consumed. The third bowl is dried and put away. Everyone begins together and ends together. Sixty people are fed in forty-five minutes with no waste, no leftovers, and no dishes to wash.

But oryoki is not just a prescribed form or a ritual. It is a state of mind. It's not about three bowls or five bowls. It's not about chanting and bowing and bells. It's a state of consciousness. Because food is life it is of utmost importance that we receive it with deepest gratitude. When we eat we consume life. Whether it's cabbages or cows, it's life. There isn't a meal that's taken by any creature, large or small, on the face of this great earth that's not done except at the expense of another creature's life. That's the nature of life on the planet Earth. We nourish and sustain each other with our lives. How can we not be grateful for the life that sustains us? How can we not wish to give back to the ten thousand things that which we receive? And it's in that process that the sacredness of taking a meal and the truth of the ten thousand dharmas is revealed.

In the Vimalakirti Nirdesha Sutra it is said that when a person is enlightened in their eating, all things are enlightened as well. If all dharmas are nondual, the person in their eating is also non-dual. Master Dogen elaborates:

> Indeed Dharma is identified with one's eating, and one's eating is identified with Dharma. For this reason, if Dharma is the Dharma-nature, then a meal also is the Dharma-nature.

Dharma is one of the Three Treasures of Buddhism: the Buddha, Dharma, and Sangha. Buddha treasure is the historical Buddha, but it is also all sentient beings. Buddha means "Enlightened One." Dharma is the teachings of the Buddha, and at the same time,

Dharma is the ten thousand things—the whole phenomenal universe. And Sangha is the community of practitioners of the Buddha's Dharma, and at once, all sentient beings. So Buddha, Dharma, and Sangha are at once the individual and the whole phenomenal universe. When Dogen talks about Dharma nature here, he is talking about the teachings and the whole phenomenal universe.

> For this reason, if Dharma is the Dharma nature, then a meal also is the Dharma nature. If Dharma is Thusness, food is likewise Thusness. If Dharma is one mind, a meal is also one mind. If Dharma is enlightenment, food is enlightenment. Therefore the act of eating constitutes the truth of all dharmas. This can fully be comprehended only by and among buddhas. At the very moment we eat, we are possessed of ultimate reality, essence, substance, energy, activity, causation. So Dharma is eating and eating is Dharma. And this Dharma is enjoyed by buddhas of past and future. This eating is full of holy joy and ecstasy.

"At the very moment we eat, we are possessed of ultimate reality, essence, substance, energy, activity, causation." We merge with the whole phenomenal universe. We're in a dynamic relationship with it. If the water on this mountain were tagged with heavy hydrogen, in a very short period of time you would find it in the plants that are growing in the garden, in the grasses, deer, raccoons, and the eagles. You'd find it in the people. It'd be in our breath and our urine. It would be in the water that flows to New York City. It would be in Alaska, New Zealand, and Japan. Each time a person would come here and consume a meal with this water, they would take it back to wherever they go and introduce it into the incredible biological equilibrium of that ecosystem. In a very short period of time, it would reach everywhere. That's the way it is. It does reach everywhere. We reach everywhere. Past, present, and future. There's no way that we can separate ourselves from this earth, from this universe.

When we take a meal, we enter into the process of merging with everything that surrounds us. When we defecate, we enter into the process of merging with everything that surrounds us. When we breathe in and out, that dynamic equilibrium that is the Diamond Net of Indra is activated, and we become part of the whole universe. When we realize it with our mind, we merge. So eating becomes a celebration of the Dharma, with no separation between eating and the samadhi of self-fulfillment, the samadhi of play, the samadhi of self-fulfilling activity.

We take our food in a bowl. We call the bowl the Buddha's bowl. Master Dogen said:

> The Buddha-bowl is not an artifact, it nei-
> ther arises nor perishes, neither comes nor
> goes, neither gains nor loses. It is not con-
> cerned with past, present, or future. This
> bowl is called the miraculous utensil.

Miraculous because it's used in a miraculous event, at a miraculous time, by a miraculous person. On this account, when a miraculous event is realized, there is a miraculous bowl. There is no need to search for the miraculous. We're surrounded by it, interpenetrated by it. Our very life is a manifestation of that miracu-lousness. When we acknowledge that the food we eat comes from the efforts of all sentient beings, past and present, we immediately identify with that Great Net of Indra.

What prevents us from identifying with the universe is what we are incessantly clinging to, all the stuff we carry around with us that constantly reaf-firms the illusion of a self that appears separate from others. That is the basic cause of all pain and suffer-ing. We need to take off the blinders that restrict our

vision, set down the pack filled with all the things that we carry. Then, free of any encumbrance, we can journey straight ahead, deep into the recesses of the hundred thousand mountains and valleys.

You don't need to take provisions with you. You need to take a risk. Take a chance. Trust yourself. Trust the process. The hundred thousand mountains and valleys are the ups and downs of life—the world of phenomena, of conflict, of barriers. Go unencumbered. Be the barrier. Let the teaching reveal itself. And you'll find that among falling blossoms and flowing streams, no trace of passing remains: no trace because there's a total merging with the ten thousand things. There are no tracks; there's no wake. There's just the ten thousand things manifesting themselves as this very body and mind; the body and mind of the Buddha; the body and mind of all sentient beings. Your body and mind.

QUESTIONS

AND

ANSWERS

*I live alone and am able to work a lot of practice into my life, and
I worry that I'm becoming very rigid.*

Discipline is different from rigidity. There is a
tremendous difference between being locked into
something and being personally disciplined. If you
lose your sense of humor, lose your flexibility, take a
close look at what you're doing. Are you looking for
control or for freedom? Attaining complete freedom
is implicit in this practice. That's what should be
coming out of your zazen. Instead of tightening, you
should be loosening up. I've had students who were
some of the most tight-assed people you've ever seen

in your life and by the time they'd finished a year of residency, they'd loosened up considerably. If that's not happening, you need to look at how you practice.

How can I bring some of the support I find at the monastery into my daily life?

When I was a lay practitioner unable to live at the monastery, I used to have a tape recorder plugged into my alarm clock radio. When the alarm went off, it triggered a sequence of sounds that mark the wake up at the monastery. I would get up and do my routine exactly the same way it was done at the monastery. I was rushing for my cup of coffee to get into the zendo five minutes before zazen was supposed to start. There was nobody telling me what to do. I was being run by this little tape recorder, but I did it. It was a way of disciplining myself. There are all kinds of tricks that you can work out that are appropriate to your own situation.

Could you please comment on the function of sacred space in one's home?

The sacred space within your household is the heart of everything else that follows. That space doesn't need to be elaborate. It's just a place that you can go to that creates a kind of attitude of mind that's

conducive to centering yourself and coming home to your practice. It can be a corner of a room. Put a rug down and set up an altar that is meaningful to you. When you are going to enter that space wear your robe if you have one. If not, use clothing that you wear only for the purpose of zazen, something comfortable that you associate your sitting with.

Sometimes that space just evolves through your sitting. You do zazen and the space grows around you. I had been sitting for a couple of years, but then one evening, out of the blue, I offered incense. I propped up a stick of incense in an ashtray. I had no altar. I used to go into my office and sit there on a folded pillow. On this particular day, when I offered that incense, I had this overwhelming sense that this is what I would be doing for the rest of my life. It was a sacred moment for me. Then I got a little romantic, and I started saving the ashes from every time I sat. And it began to accumulate until there was enough to hold up my stick of incense. When I started sitting at a training center, I took some of the ashes from the main altar there. I did the same thing at each place that I studied. I took that with me to our monastery and distributed it in every altar. Now each altar has a couple of particles of the original ash from the sitting that day, over thirty years ago. That sense of personal significance is important. If it means something to you it will support your practice and it will touch others. Total strangers walk into our zendo and get a sense that this is a place where people have been sitting and really working on themselves. That dedication and significance communicate very clearly.

How can you create a supportive environment at work where the general tendency is to be overwhelmed by the bustle and confusion?

When I was working as a scientist, I was a closet Buddhist. Twenty-five years ago Buddhism wasn't as popular and accepted as it is now, particularly in the world of science. I thought that if any of my coworkers found out that I was practicing, that would have cast doubt on my ability as a researcher. So I kept it quiet. Nobody knew that I used to go off to a monastery and sit zazen at home. But I wanted to bring my practice into the workplace. I began to see that I was living a dualistic life. There was the very sacred and spiritual aspect of it, and the craziness that would emerge when I walked through the door of my department. Whenever things got really crazy around me, I would use a picture of Jizo Bodhisattva that I placed on my desk as a reminder of sanity, a place that was untouchable. You can always do that. You can create a sanctuary even in a workplace, even if you don't

have a desk or an office. There's a place you can find to do that, even if it's in your wallet. You can take a photo out, look at it, and remind yourself what your life is really about; that it's not all of the turmoil; that it's different, and you want to make it different. You remind yourself of your vow and commitment to realize yourself. And it'll bring you home every time.

What is the relationship of the different forms we encounter in liturgy to the essence of Zen teachings?

Our tendency is to think in terms of form. Form is necessary for the purpose of training, but behind the form is a principle. Oryoki is a state of consciousness, it's not five bowls and a napkin and chanting aloud. It's a state of consciousness. Once you've connected with that state of consciousness, then oryoki is truly yours. Then, in a moment of silence, in a restaurant, without drawing attention to yourself, you can do oryoki. When the meal is put in front of you, you can identify with it, express the gatha of receiving a meal and then take the meal.

I have a problem with chanting out loud. There are a lot of other people living close by and I get embarrassed.

You don't have to chant so loud! You can do it silently. Invoking has little to do with the volume of your voice. It has all to do with the state of your mind. When I do my service at dawn, my son is still asleep, so I chant silently, focusing completely on the words.

Are there shorter versions of the Meal Gatha?

There's a Short Meal Gatha which says:

We receive this food in gratitude to all beings
Who have helped bring it to our table,
And vow to respond in turn to those in need
With wisdom and compassion.

It's a very simple gatha that any family can do, and it's broad enough that it should be acceptable within any religious context. It's essentially an expression of gratitude and a vow of wisdom and compassion.

How are dedications used in the context of home liturgy?

The dedication to the Heart Sutra is very similar to the one that we use at the monastery. "Buddha nature pervades the whole universe, existing right here now. In reciting the Heart Sutra we dedicate its merits to the Great Master Shakyamuni Buddha, to the successive great masters, and especially to the health, well-being, and peace of (your family.)"

I do a family service first thing in the morning, every day. To my dharma family—the lineage, my teacher and my dharma brothers and sisters, and to my personal family—my children and grandchildren. The dedication continues, "May our lives be ones of wisdom and compassion, and may we realize the Buddha Way together." The dedication connects you with your spiritual and genetic family, it reaffirms your practice, and it reminds you what your life is about. It's a good way to start the day, following your morning zazen.

When do you use a memorial service?

The Family Memorial Service is used on the anniversary of the death of a family member. It's a good way to reconnect with them. You chant Emmei Jukku Kannon Gyo, and then the dedication. In the dedication, the *udumbara* is a mythical flower that blooms once in a hundred thousand kalpas; a very unusual event.

Is there a reason why Emmei Jukku Kannon Gyo is used for a memorial service?

This chant invokes Kannon Bodhisattva, the bodhisattva of compassion. She has ten thousand arms

that are constantly reaching out to alleviate suffering. Her name in Sanskrit, Avalokiteshvara, literally means "hearer of the cries of the world." She always responds by taking a form appropriate to the circumstances. She may manifest as a motorist who stops to give aid to another motorist, or as a tattooed biker in a saloon who is keeping two guys from killing each other. The heart of Kannon Bodhisattva is the heart of each one of us. The potential for wisdom and compassion exists in each one of us. When it comes to the surface and begins to function, we begin to manifest Kannon Bodhisattva.

Master Hakuin said that just to chant Emmei Jukku Kannon Gyo causes all kinds of marvelous things to occur. And indeed they do occur, but it's not magic. It's you manifesting the spirit of compassion that you already have. Each one of us carries the whole spectrum of human potential; we can be killers or lovers, and we can be rude or compassionate. How we practice our lives is what manifests as our lives.

Why is the Gatha of Atonement so central to all of the ceremonies and liturgy in Zen?

The Gatha of Atonement connects us with the precepts. A good time to chant the Gatha is at the end of a day, when you may have some regrets about your actions. You are identifying with, and taking responsibility for the karma that you created so that you are empowered to let it go, and to go on. You cannot truly let go until you have taken full responsibility for your actions, until you have atoned.

When do you use the Work Gatha?

It's a way to start your day of work. You want to dedicate what you're about to do to all beings. When you dedicate your work, it changes your attitude about it. It also helps you examine what it is that you're doing, and how you're doing it. And it begins to make conscious the whole question of right livelihood.

Is "giving" an adequate translation of the word dana*?*

"Compassionate giving" captures it better. But there's still more to dana. Dana is a *paramita*, a perfection. There's a sense of giving and receiving implicit in dana. It never goes one way.

I never heard the Conflict Resolution Service done at the monastery. What is its purpose?

If you need to deal with a conflict, this is a good way to go into it. If both parties involved in a conflict are willing to take refuge in the Three Treasures, that sets a healthy groundwork for real communication and resolution to happen. You are talking a common language.

When we are finishing a service, we conclude with the refrain "All Buddhas." Why?

"All buddhas throughout space and time, all bodhisattvas, mahasattvas, maha prajna paramita." A Buddha is an enlightened being. Space and time includes all space and time, back through endless eons in the past and into the future. There have been many buddhas and we're identifying with all of them. Also, all of the bodhisattvas and mahasattvas—those beings who have given their lives with wisdom and compassion to help other people. "Maha prajna paramita" is the great wisdom of the other shore; the crossing over to the other shore. So we're identifying with those people and our own transformation.

It seems sort of strange that within practice some things are holy and some aren't. There's a saying about "when you're cold burn the Buddha." Yet when you go to the bathroom you hang your rakusu *up with total respect. How do we decide what is the right attitude?*

First of all, keep in mind what Master Dogen said about this: "Those who regard the mundane as a hindrance to practice only understand that in the mundane nothing is sacred; they have not yet understood that in sacredness nothing is mundane." Once you understand sacredness, you understand that it reaches everywhere. But, also keep in mind that teachers, in teaching, respond to specific situations; to particular time, place, and position. A monk asked Zhaozhou, "Does a dog have Buddha nature?" Zhaozhou said, "No." Another monk came and asked Zhaozhou the same question. Zhaozhou said, "Yes." Zhaozhou expressed the truth in both situations. The teacher who burned the wooden buddha statue and was warming his butt next to the fire was responding to people who had become attached to liturgy and iconography. They thought that the form was the reality. In this country, at this time, everybody is ready to burn buddhas. We need to learn to bow to the buddha. We need to learn to respect the inanimate. We need to see that the teachings are everywhere. It's a very different lesson. When we reach a point when liturgy and form are second nature to us, and we are tightly wrapped up in them, then we'll start burning buddhas, rakusus, and robes.

Why is it so much harder to maintain a vital Zen practice at home as compared to the monastery?

Keep in mind that what you are doing at home is essentially the same as what you do when you come to train at the monastery. We all get up in the morning, get washed, do zazen. We have breakfast, and do a little caretaking—pick up the stuff you didn't take care of last night, or wash the dishes that are in the sink. Then go off to work. Coming back from work, we eat dinner, read a bit, do evening zazen, closing the day. So why does rounded practice work at the monastery and is so difficult at home, even though the same principles apply? One major difference is that at the monastery you have a supporting cast— the sangha. Still, the key to understanding this discrepancy is to see how you appreciate what practice is. People say, "Everything I do is practice." That's easy to say, but how much of your life is real practice? How do you engage your life? How much do you *want* to engage your life?

DAILY

LITURGY

Introduction to Daily Liturgy

The home dweller liturgy is designed to function for an individual practitioner or a small group. Services should be done in front of an altar, facing it. You can offer a stick of incense, touching it to your forehead before placing it in the incense bowl. Every service begins and ends with three bows. The bows may be standing or full prostrations. During a service, hands are brought into gassho, a gesture where the palms are held together few inches in front of you, with the tips of your fingers on the level of your nose.

Depending on your living circumstances, chant-ing can be done aloud or, if you need to respect others' presence and be unobtrusive, you can chant quietly, under your breath or silently, in your mind. The volume is less important than your attentive-ness and focus on the chanting. The chanting is done in a low monotone, staying on the same note, and maintaining an even, moderate rhythm. Try to chant from your *hara*, the physical and spiritual cen-ter of the body, a place two to three inches below your navel.

The following are simple guidelines on how different chants included in this manual can be in-corporated into your daily practice. Explore the pos-sibilities, keeping foremost in mind your intent, the relevance of what you are taking up, and the practi-calities of your living situation.

It is recommended that the Family Service takes place each day. The Heart Sutra is chanted first with its dedication following, in the dedication filling in the name of your family. All Buddhas is chanted to conclude the service.

The Verse of the Vestment of Compassion can be chanted three times at the end of morning zazen. Similarly the Four Boddhisattva Vows are tradition-ally chanted at the conclusion of evening zazen, as a rededication of our practice.

The Family Memorial Service acknowledges the anniversary of the passing of a family member, and the Healing Service is used to nourish the health and well-being of a family member or a friend suffering a life-threatening illness. Emmei Jukku Kannon Gyo may be used with the appropriate dedication, concluding with All Buddhas.

The Work Gatha normally precedes the day's work, focusing our mind on our life's efforts, and the Meal Gatha or Short Meal Gatha are an expression of receiving, giving, and gratitude, and can be done before meals.

A Conflict Resolution Service is a good way to begin work on the resolution of differences. The Gatha of Atonement is chanted three times. If both parties are practitioners, this can be done together.

For more comments on some of these services, see the Questions and Answers section of this book.

In practicing these services it is important that they be conducted with awareness and a reverential attitude, so that they don't deteriorate into meaningless rituals. If they are practiced well, engaged with an open mind and heart, they are certain to nurture and to reveal how in sacredness nothing is mundane.

Creating a Home Altar

A typical altar consists of a central image of a buddha or one of the bodhisattvas. Directly in front of the image is a cup filled with water, and in front of that an incense bowl in which incense sticks are offered. The incense bowl can be filled with ashes, sand, or rice—substances that can support an incense stick. Facing the altar, a candle is on the right, and live flowers on the left. The water, incense, burning candle, and flowers represent the four elements of water, air, fire, and earth.

In setting up a home altar, try to use components that are meaningful to you. If necessary, let the altar evolve over time. Creating a sacred space means to bring sensitivity, proper attitude, and awareness to the physical space that you are entering. Maintaining a sacred space is to maintain those qualities of body and mind. Take care of the altar. Keep the flowers fresh, water cup filled, the area clean. Let the altar be a concrete reminder to you of your intent to awaken and take care of all beings.

Maha Prajna Paramita Heart Sutra

Avalokiteshvara Bodhisattva, doing deep
Prajna Paramita, clearly saw emptiness of
all the five conditions, thus completely
relieving misfortune and pain.

O Shariputra, form is no other than emptiness,
emptiness no other than form. Form is
exactly emptiness, emptiness exactly form.
Sensation, conception, discrimination,
awareness are likewise like this.

O Shariputra, all dharmas are forms of emptiness; not born, not destroyed, not stained,
not pure, without loss, without gain.

So in emptiness there is no form; no sensation,
conception, discrimination, awareness; no
eye, ear, nose, tongue, body, mind; no color,
sound, smell, taste, touch, phenomena; no
realm of sight, no realm of consciousness,
no ignorance and no end to ignorance, no
old age and death and no end to old age and
death, no suffering, no cause of suffering,
no extinguishing, no path, no wisdom, and
no gain.

No gain, and thus the bodhisattva lives Prajna
  Paramita, with no hindrance in the mind; no
  hindrance, therefore no fear. Far beyond
  deluded thoughts; this is nirvana.
All past, present, and future buddhas live
  Prajna Paramita and therefore attain *anuttara
  samyak-sambodhi.*
Therefore know Prajna Paramita is the great
  mantra, the vivid mantra, the best mantra,
  the unsurpassable mantra. It completely
  clears all pain. This is the truth, not a lie.
So set forth the Prajna Paramita mantra, set
  forth this mantra and say,
Gate! Gate! Paragate! Parasamgate! Bodhi svaha!
Prajna Heart Sutra.

Heart Sutra Dedication

Buddha Nature pervades the whole universe
　　existing right here now.
In reciting the Heart Sutra, we dedicate its
　　merits to:
The Great Master Shakyamuni Buddha,
The successive Great Masters,
And especially to the health, well being, and
　　peace of the _____ Family.
May our lives be ones of wisdom and
　　compassion,
And may we realize the Buddha Way together.

Emmei Jukku Kannon Gyo

Kan ze on na mu butsu yo butsu u in yo butsu
  u en bup po so en jo raku ga jo cho nen kan
  ze on bo nen kan ze on nen nen ju shin ki
  nen nen fu ri shin.

Kan ze on na mu butsu yo butsu u in yo butsu
  u en bup po so en jo raku ga jo cho nen kan
  ze on bo nen kan ze on nen nen ju shin ki
  nen nen fu ri shin.

Kan ze on na mu butsu yo butsu u in yo butsu
  u en bup po so en jo raku ga jo cho nen kan
  ze on bo nen kan ze on nen nen ju shin ki
  nen nen fu ri shin.

Family Memorial Service Dedication

In reciting the Emmei Jukku Kannon Gyo, and
    in offering flowers, candlelight, and incense,
We dedicate its merits to: The memory of
    _____, on this his/her memorial day.
May the udumbara bloom in endless spring,
And may we realize the Buddha Way together.

Healing Service Dedication

In reciting the Emmei Jukku Kannon Gyo,
We dedicate its merits to: The health and
    well being of _____.
May she/he heal all her/his ills,
And may we realize the Buddha Way together.

Meal Gatha

First, seventy-two labors brought us this food;
We should know how it comes to us.
Second, as we receive this offering, we should
    consider whether our virtue and practice
    deserve it.
Third, as we desire the natural order of mind
    to be free from clinging, we must be free
    from greed.
Fourth, to support our life we take this food.
Fifth, to attain our way we take this food.

First, this food is for the Three Treasures.
Second, it is for our teachers, parents, nation,
    and all sentient beings.
Third, it is for all beings in the six worlds.
Thus, we eat this food with everyone.
We eat to stop all evil, to practice good, to save
    all sentient beings, and to accomplish our
    Buddha Way.

Short Meal Gatha

We receive this food in gratitude to all beings
Who have helped to bring it to our table,
And vow to respond in turn to those in need
With wisdom and compassion.

Gatha of Atonement
(Chanted three times)

All evil karma ever committed by me since
of old.
On account of my beginningless greed, anger,
and ignorance.
Born of my body, mouth, and thought.
Now I atone for it all.

Verse of the Vestment of Compassion
(Chanted three times)

Vast is the robe of liberation,
A formless field of benefaction.
I wear the Tathagata's teachings,
Saving all sentient beings.

The Four Bodhisattva Vows

Sentient beings are numberless; I vow to
   save them.
Desires are inexhaustible; I vow to put an end
   to them.
The Dharmas are boundless; I vow to master
   them.
The Buddha Way is unattainable; I vow to
   attain it.

Work Gatha

Gate! Gate! Paragate! Parasamgate! Bodhi
    Svaha.
Gate! Gate! Paragate! Parasamgate! Bodhi
    Svaha.
Gate! Gate! Paragate! Parasamgate! Bodhi
    Svaha.
Gate! Gate! Paragate! Parasamgate! Bodhi
    Svaha.
Gate! Gate! Paragate! Parasamgate! Bodhi
    Svaha.
Prajna Paramita.

Work Gatha Dedication

May this compassionate Dana
Be extended to all sentient beings.
And may our sincere vows
To accomplish the Buddha Way
Be realized together.

All Buddhas

All Buddhas throughout space and time
All Bodhisattvas, Mahasattvas
Maha Prajna Paramita

Appendix

THE DOOR
TO AWARENESS:
A DHARMA DISCOURSE

A dharma discourse, or teisho, *is a formal talk on a particular aspect of the Zen teachings. It is not an intellectual presentation or philosophical explanation, but a direct expression of the spirit of Zen by the teacher to his or her students.*

Dharma discourses generally deal with a Zen koan—a seemingly paradoxical statement or question that challenges our understanding of who we are, what the nature of the self is, and what the activity of our life expresses. There are many commentaries on classical Zen koans by both Eastern and Western masters currently available in

English. These texts provide access to the way Zen study has been brought to life through the lineage of realized teachers that began with Shakyamuni Buddha twenty-five hundred years ago.

Dharma discourses are said to be "dark to the mind but radiant to the heart." They require that we open ourselves to what initially may appear to be an intentionally confusing and frustrating way of using language. At Zen Mountain Monastery, dharma discourses are offered following formal sitting periods, and they are received with the same spirit and focus emphasized in zazen.

Because reading is essentially solitary, the intimacy of heart-to-heart, mind-to-mind communication that characterizes dharma discourses may be even more accessible to you as a reader. Please read the words that follow with your heart and give them your full attention, letting go of all the thoughts and analysis that are part of our habitual way of using our minds.

The practice of reading or hearing a dharma discourse does not involve acquiring information, but lies instead in the direct and personal experience of the awakened mind. Our job is to get out of our own way, so that we can experience what has always been present in each and every one of us.

Yangshan Chanting the Sutras*

Main Case

One day when Yangshan was a novice, he was reciting a sutra.

Shaozhou Ruyuan said, "Huiji, your chanting
sounds like weeping."†

Yangshan said, "This is how I do it, Master. I
wonder how you would do it."‡

Shaozhou just looked around.

Yangshan said, "If you chant like that, how is it
different from weeping?"§

Shaozhou was silenced and walked away.

Commentary

Although Yangshan is feisty and slippery, he is still a
willing student. But alas, Shaozhou, in trying to respond, slips and falls. Nonetheless, Yangshan should
understand that if chanting lacks spiritual power, although it may pass from mouth to ear, it inevitably

---

* Dharma Discourse by John Daido Loori Roshi from *The True Dharma Eye: Master Dogen's Three Hundred Koans* (Boston: Shambhala, 2005), Case 246.

† He diminishes the man.

‡ When you press down on a floating gourd, it rolls over and pops back up.

§ He diminishes the man.

fails to pierce the heart. How does one manifest spiritual power that can pierce the heart?

The attainment of spiritual power simply depends on penetrating the principle and fully engaging the ten thousand dharmas. Master Zhaozhou said, "People, just sit and penetrate the principle." All practices, such as eating, working, prostrating, and chanting the sutras are to be done in the spirit of zazen. If you wish to understand this kind of spiritual power, you must first understand the dharma of chanting. An ancient once said, "If it's not present in your mind, your mouth chants empty words." Chanting, like invoking, means to call to mind. Chanting and invoking have to do with thought and not with language.

Be that as it may, say a word of Zen for Shaozhou in answer to Yangshan's question, "I wonder how you would do it?"

Capping Verse

> The talkative teacher can't open his mouth,
>   the tricky student misses the point.
> Spiritual powers and their wondrous
>   functioning—
> hauling water and carrying firewood.

Some forty or fifty years ago, when the dharma first came to America, most of the Japanese teachers training Western students focused on what was easiest for them to convey: zazen. As a result, the liturgical services that were handed down were either extremely simplified or nonexistent. Zen Buddhism is rich in liturgy, however, so it's a shame to be satisfied with only a smattering.

The first thing we need to understand about liturgy is that it's a practice. This means that we have to do it; we have to fully participate in it. Liturgy is not a spectator sport—neither is zazen, or work practice, or any of the other gates of training—and neither is life, for that matter. We should look at the areas of our lives where we're just treading water and start swimming. We should engage them fully, just like Zhaozhou says: "Practice the principle."

This koan begins, "One day when Yangshan was a novice, he was reciting a sutra." Yangshan was a successor to the great master Guishan and the cofounder of the Guiyang school of Zen. This koan took place when Yangshan was still young, as you can see from the interaction.

"Shaozhou Ruyuan said, 'Huiji, your chanting sounds like weeping.'" Shaozhou was one of Mazu's eighty-four enlightened successors, but very little else is known about him. Huiji was Yangshan's nickname. "Weeping" could also be translated as "wailing," the kind that you would do at a funeral, for example. "Yangshan said, 'This is how I do it, Master. I wonder, how would you do it?' Shaozhou just looked around." It's as if he were looking for an answer somewhere. "Yangshan said, 'If you chant like that, how is it different from weeping?' Shaozhou was silenced and walked away."

The commentary says, "Although Yangshan is feisty and slippery, he is still a willing student. But alas, Shaozhou, in trying to respond, slips and falls. Nonetheless, Yangshan should understand that if chanting lacks spiritual power, although it may pass from mouth to ear, it inevitably fails to pierce the heart. How does one manifest spiritual power that can pierce the heart?"

Spiritual power is *ki* or *chi.* It's energy. It's the ki in *joriki,* the power of concentration. Ki is what's developed in zazen, it's what functions in work, in art, in seeing, in hearing, in feeling, in loving. The Chinese say that if a painting doesn't contain ki, it's dead. If a work of art has ki, it inevitably reflects the vitality of spirit that is the essence of life itself. The commentary, on the other hand, is referring to activity that lacks ki: "Nonetheless, Yangshan should understand that if chanting lacks spiritual power, although it may pass from mouth to ear, it inevitably fails to pierce the heart." This kind of chanting has no power, no ki. So what kind of chanting *does* pierce the heart? And more important, how do we practice it?

Analysis doesn't reveal what's happening in liturgy, and it doesn't free us. Instead it paralyzes us. Liturgy is experiential; we have to do it to connect with it. We have to actively engage it. We have to study it, question it, and probe its depths. It can't be just dead words. We have to really feel it and bring to it our own life energy, our own ki. Only then can it be of any use to us in our everyday lives.

The next question in the commentary is "How does one manifest spiritual power that can pierce the heart?" In Buddhism we speak of six kinds of spiritual power: first, the power of mystical transmigration; that is, the ability to move from place to place, or from one body to another. The second is the power to read people's minds. The third is the power of supernatural vision, to be able to see things that are beyond the senses. The fourth is the power of supernatural hearing, to hear beyond sound. The fifth is the power to know past lives. And finally, there is the power to end excesses, to know how to let go. In Indian metaphysics there are volumes written about these six powers, but whenever disciples would ask the Buddha about any of them, he would always bring them back to the moment: What is here right now? That is the true mystical experience. Drinking tea, washing your face—the miracle of each and every breath. So how do we manifest this spiritual power? How do we attain it?

"The attainment of spiritual power simply depends on penetrating the principle and fully engaging the ten thousand dharmas." In actual fact, these two statements are identical. Penetrating the principle and fully engaging the ten thousand dharmas are one and the same reality. What is the principle? It's the essential matter, the nature of reality, the nature of the self, *yourself.* When we realize the nature of the self, we realize the nature of the universe. To fully engage the ten thousand dharmas, that too is the whole phenomenal universe. This is the whole point of zazen. It's the whole point of liturgy. It's the whole point of practice.

"Master Zhaozhou said, 'People, just sit and penetrate the principle.' All practices, such as eating, working, prostrating, and chanting the sutras are to be done in the spirit of zazen." What is the spirit of zazen? We begin by quieting the body. We take the posture of the Buddha. That in itself starts the process. And if you sit consistently, even the most scattered mind will begin to come into accord with the body. Body and mind are one reality. They're not two separate things. We like to think of them as separate, but they're not. When the body is agitated, the

mind is agitated. When the mind is agitated, the body is agitated. We therefore begin by stilling and centering the body. How? By focusing on the hara, the physical and spiritual center of your body located about two or three fingers below the navel.

There's an interesting section in the autobiography of Master Hakuin, the reformer of the Japanese Rinzai school from which our lineage is derived. Hakuin quotes the priest Po yün, who said,

> I always keep my heart [this character could also be translated as mind] down filling my lower belly. I use it all the time— teaching students, guiding the assembly of monks, receiving visitors, during encounters in my chambers, while busily engaged in talks and lectures of various kinds—and I never use it up. Since reaching old age, I've found its benefits to be especially great.

Then Hakuin comments on this:

> How commendable! Don't Po yün's words agree with the teachings found in the *Su-wen?* "If you are tranquil and free of troubling thoughts, the primal energy will

conform. As long as you preserve that energy within, there's no place for illness to enter."

Keep in mind that when he speaks of illness, he's speaking of mental agitation as well as physical illness.

Moreover, the essence of preserving the energy within is to keep it replete and secure throughout the entire body—extending it to all three hundred and sixty joints and each of the eighty-four thousands pores of the skin. You must know that this is the ultimate secret of sustaining life.

The hara is critical in practice. It is the source of our *joriki*. Whether we're chanting, painting, working, eating, or even sleeping, the hara should be the focus of all of our activities. As the commentary says, "All practices, such as eating, working, prostrating, and chanting the sutras are to be done in the spirit of zazen"—the spirit of single-pointed attention to doing what you're doing while you're doing it.

The commentary continues: "If you wish to understand this kind of spiritual power, you must first understand the dharma of chanting." Sometimes

people think that if they're chanting louder than everyone else, then they're really doing liturgy. But it doesn't work like that. A sangha chanting together is not like a bunch of drunks singing in a bar, with every ego trying to outdo every other ego. True chanting is in complete accord with its surroundings. It comes from the hara and a mind that's focused. It manifests each individual's ki, and then creates a group ki. That's when you know that the chanting has arrived. It's very rare to hear that, but it happens. I call it "angel voices" because they don't really belong to any individual; they are sounds and overtones that harmonize with the sangha's chanting and create a whole new sound.

"An ancient once said, 'If it's not present in your mind, your mouth chants empty words.' Chanting, like invoking, means to call to mind. Chanting and invoking have to do with thought and not with language." Chanting comes from what you do with your mind, not with the words.

Bodhidharma, the founder of Zen, was once asked by a monastic, "The sutras say that someone who wholeheartedly invokes the Buddha is sure to be reborn in Western Paradise. Since this door leads to buddhahood, why seek liberation in beholding the mind?" "Beholding the mind" is Bodhidharma's term for zazen, so the monastic is essentially asking why don't we just chant the name of the Buddha instead of doing zazen? It's much easier. Bodhidharma's response was:

> Buddha means awareness, the awareness of body and mind that prevents evil from arising in either, and to invoke means to call to mind, the call constantly to mind, the rules of discipline and to follow them with all your might. This is what is meant by invoking.
>
> Invoking has to do with thought, not with language. If you use a trap to catch fish, once you succeed, you can forget the trap. And if you use language to find meaning, once you find it, you can forget language. To invoke the Buddha's name you have to understand the dharma of invoking. If it's not present in your mind, your mind chants an empty name. As long as you're troubled by the three poisons, greed, anger, and ignorance, or by thoughts of yourself, your deluded mind will keep you from seeing Buddha, and you'll only waste your effort. Chanting and invoking are worlds apart. Chanting is done with the mouth; invoking is done with the

mind. And because invoking comes from the mind, it is called the door to awareness. Chanting is centered in the mouth and it appears as sound. If you cling to appearances while searching for meaning, you won't find a thing. Thus the sages of the past cultivated introspection and not speech.

The final line of the commentary reads, "Be that as it may, say a word of Zen for Shaozhou in answer to Yangshan's question, 'I wonder how you would do it?'" Ask yourself the question, how do *I* chant the sutras? And with that, work through an answer for Yangshan, who asked, "I wonder how you would do it?"

The capping verse:

The talkative teacher can't open his mouth,
    the tricky student misses the point.
Spiritual powers and their wondrous
    functioning—
hauling water and carrying firewood.

"The talkative teacher can't open his mouth, the tricky student misses the point." Yangshan may have been slick, he may have outwitted the old man, leaving him speechless, but who lost, really? Yang-shan went off somehow thinking that it was okay to do what he did. Was it? You tell me.

"Spiritual powers and their wondrous function-ing—hauling water and carrying firewood." These last two lines are Layman Pang's, who uttered them upon his realization. He was saying that the won-drous functioning of his spiritual power was alive in each and every one of his daily activities. Isn't that what it's ultimately about? Isn't that why we practice—to see how the dharma functions in the way we live our lives, raise a child, take care of people, things, ourselves, others? Well, liturgy is a key part of this process. We should learn how to use it well. We should learn how to invoke it, not for our own bene-fit, but for the benefit of others.

Liturgy contains a profound secret that is con-stantly being revealed in the eighty-four thousand subtle gestures that make up our practice. It is the secret to world peace, the secret to social transfor-mation, to ecological harmony, to marriage and rela-tionships, the secret to raising children, dancing, chopping wood, carrying water. The secret is this in-credible dharma dance that we call life, but it must be danced to be realized. It's not the words that describe it. It's not the ideas we have about it. It's the reality itself. The dance, the bow, the voice. Liturgy should

not be an empty exhibition of form. It should be the actualization of the buddhas and ancestors of the past, present, and future. It's no small thing by any measure, so please don't take it lightly. Give life to your liturgy. Give life to the Buddha.

Glossary

ANUTTARA SAMYAK-SAMBODHI: Supreme perfect enlightenment of a complete Buddha.

ATONEMENT: Act of becoming one with; taking full responsibility.

AVALOKITESHVARA: Literally, "hearer of the cries of the world." Bodhisattva of Compassion; known in Chinese as Kuan-yin (Guanyin) and Japanese as Kannon and often depicted in female form.

BODHIDHARMA: (ca. 470–543?) Twenty-eighth patriarch of Zen in India, first patriarch of Zen in China.

BODHISATTVA: Literally, "enlightened being." One who practices the Buddha Way and compassionately postpones final enlightenment for the sake of others; the ideal of practice in Mahayana Buddhism.

BUDDHA: Literally, "awakened one." A person who has achieved complete enlightenment and thus liberation from the suffering of the phenomenal world.

Buddha nature: The Way, primary principle, universal reality; the nameless and unnameable source of all things.

Changsha: Ch'ang-sha Ching-ts'en (d. 868). Chinese Zen master. A student and successor of the great master Nan-ch'üan.

compassion: In Sanskrit, *karuna*. The manifestation of wisdom (*prajna*) as activity in the world of phenomena.

Daiosho: "Great Teacher." Term of respect for a Zen master, especially the key teachers of a lineage.

dana: "Compassionate giving"; Voluntary giving, considered in Buddhism as one of the most important virtues; one of the six paramitas, or perfections.

dharani: A brief chant consisting of fundamental sounds that carry no extrinsic meaning.

Dharma wheel: Symbol of the Buddhist teachings. Commonly depicted as wheel with eight spokes, representing the Eightfold Path of the Buddha.

Dharma: 1) Universal truth or law; 2) the Buddha's teachings; 3) all phenomena that make up reality.

Diamond Net of Indra: Metaphor for the interdependent nature of reality, conceived as a net of diamonds spread throughout all space and time, with each diamond reflecting all others simultaneously.

Dogen: Dogen Kigen (1200–1253). Founder of the Soto school of Zen in Japan; established Eiheiji, the principal Soto training monastery; author of the *Shobogenzo*, an important collection of Dharma essays.

DOKUSAN/DAISAN: Private interviews with the teacher during which students present and clarify their understanding of the Dharma.

EIHEI SHINGI: A manual written by Dogen to guide practice at Eiheiji and establish the rules of monastic life.

EIHEIJI: One of the two principal training monasteries of the Soto school in Japan (the other is Sojiji), founded by Dogen in 1243.

EMPTINESS: A translation of the Sanskrit term *shunyata*. Central principle of Buddhism that recognizes the impermanence and interdependence of all composite entities, without reifying nothingness. Resolution of all dualities. Comprehension of emptiness through the intuitive wisdom of PRAJNA is the basis of realization.

ENLIGHTENMENT: Direct experience of one's true nature.

FOUR BODHISATTVA VOWS: Vows taken by the bodhisattvas, expressing commitment to postpone their own enlightenment until all beings are liberated from delusion; they are chanted at the end of each day at Zen monasteries.

GASSHO: Gesture of bringing one's hands together, palm to palm, embodying the identity of all dualities.

GATHA: Brief verse that presents the Dharma teachings in terse, pithy wording; frequently chanted.

GOLDEN AGE OF ZEN: Period in T'ang-dynasty China, roughly the ninth century, when Zen flourished under such masters as Zhaozhou, Deshan, Linji, and others.

HAKUIN: Hakuin Ekaku (1689–1769). One of the most important Zen masters in the Japanese Rinzai tradition. He systematized koan study and revitalized the practice of zazen.

HEART SUTRA: English translation of the Mahaprajnaparamita Hridaya Sutra. Brief sutra distilling the essence of the vast *Prajnaparamita* teachings. One of the most important of all Mahayana sutras for its teaching on emptiness, it is chanted daily in Buddhist monasteries and centers around the world.

HOME DWELLER: A lay practitioner of Buddhism, in contrast to a "home leaver," or monastic.

INKIN: A handbell struck to mark specific points during a Buddhist service.

JIZO: A bodhisattva known in Sanskrit as Kshitigarbha; protector of children, travelers, and beings suffering in the hell realms.

KANNON: See Avalokiteshvara.

KARMA: The universal law of cause and effect, linking an action's underlying intention to that action's consequences; it equates the actions of body, speech, and thought as potential sources of karmic consequences.

KESA: A Buddhist monk's outer robe, a physical representation of the monastic vows.

KOAN: An apparently paradoxical statement or question used in Zen training to induce in the student an intense level of doubt, allowing them to cut through conventional and conditioned descriptions of reality and see directly into their true nature.

KUAN YIN: See Avalokiteshvara.

MAHAKASHYAPA: Disciple and first successor of Shakyamuni Buddha.

MAHASATTVA: Literally, "Great being." A great bodhisattva.

MAITREYA BUDDHA: Literally, "Loving One." Buddha of the Future.

MANJUSHRI: Bodhisattva of Wisdom. Frequently depicted wielding the sword of *prajna*, which cuts through all delusion.

MANTRA: A syllable or sequence of syllables imbued with spiritual power and significance, though frequently without logical, conceptual meaning.

MOKUGYO: Literally, "wooden fish." A wooden drum, decorated with stylized fish, used to keep time during chanting.

NIRVANA: Union with the absolute; in Zen it is essential to realize that samsara is nirvana, form is emptiness, and that all beings are innately perfect from the outset.

OM: A mantra or "seed syllable" inherited by Buddhism from the Hindu tradition; it represents the totality of existence, the presence of the absolute within the relative world of phenomena.

ORYOKI: "Containing just enough"; the set of bowls, and by extension, the ceremonial meals eaten in Zen monasteries.

PARAMITAS: Perfections; virtues of attitude and behavior cultivated by bodhisattvas in the course of their development, necessary on the path of transcendence or realization; "reaching the other shore." The six paramitas are generosity, discipline, patience, exertion, meditation, and wisdom.

PRAJNA: Wisdom; not that which is possessed, but that which is directly and thoroughly experienced. Intuitive insight that cannot be expressed in concepts or in intellectual terms; penetration of the true nature of reality, which is emptiness.

RAKUSU: A bib-shaped garment that is an abbreviated version of the kesa worn by monks; it indicates that the wearer has vowed to uphold the Buddhist precepts.

ROSHI: "Venerable master"; title of Zen teachers.

SAMSARA: Existence prior to liberation, conditioned by the three attitudes of greed, anger, and ignorance and marked by continuous rebirths.

SANGHA: 1) The community of Buddhist practitioners; 2) all sentient and insentient beings.

SEVENTY-TWO LABORS: The seventy-two labors referred to in the Meal Gatha were the various service positions and tasks sustaining a traditional Zen monastery and its sangha.

SHAKYAMUNI BUDDHA: Siddhartha Gautama, the historical Buddha and the founder of Buddhism; he was a prince of the Shakya clan, living in northern India in the sixth century B.C.E.

SHARIPUTRA: One of the ten great original disciples of the Buddha.

SESSHIN: Literally, "collecting the mind." An intensive, silent Zen retreat, typically lasting from one or two days to a full week.

SIX WORLDS: Also known as the Six Realms. The various modes of existence making up samsara, or the phenomenal world: the realms of gods, humans, wrathful titans, animals, hungry ghosts, and hell.

SUTRA: Narrative text consisting chiefly of the discourses and teachings of the Buddha.

TATHAGATA: "Thus-come one," one of the titles of the Buddha, referring to one who has attained perfect enlightenment, suchness.

TENZO: The chief cook of a monastery; usually a senior monk who uses the context of food preparation and serving as skillful means for teaching those working with him or her.

THREE PILLARS OF PRACTICE: The essential components of the Zen path of realization—great doubt, great faith, and great perseverance.

THREE TREASURES: Buddha, Dharma, and Sangha; one who is awakened, the true teachings, and the group of people living in accord with the teachings; the Treasures are also known as the places of refuge for Buddhist practitioners.

TRANSMISSION: Complete, mind-to-mind merging of the teacher and the student; the confirmation of a student's realization.

UDUMBARA: A mythical flower that blooms once in a hundred thousand eons.

UPAYA: Skillful means; forms that the teachings take, reflecting their appropriateness to the circumstances in which they appear.

VESTMENT OF COMPASSION: The kesa, or monk's outer robe, worn across one shoulder. By extension, the Buddha's teachings.

VIMALAKIRTI NIRDESHA SUTRA: An important Mahayana sutra teaching the bodhisattva path. The name is drawn from the main character, Vimalakirti, a layman portrayed as the embodiment of the bodhisattva ideal.

VULTURE PEAK: Mount Gridhrakuta, a peak in India said to be the site of the Buddha's preaching of the Lotus Sutra and of his transmission of the teaching to his successor Mahakashyapa.

WISDOM: see prajna.

YASUTANI ROSHI: Hakuun Ryoko Yasutani (1885–1973). Important modern Japanese Zen master, active in bringing the Zen teachings to the West.

ZAZEN: The formal seated meditation that is the core of Zen practice.

ZENDO: Meditation hall.

ZHAOZHOU: Zhaozhou Congshen (778–897), one of the most important Chinese masters in the history of Zen; originator of the koan Mu.

Books by John Daido Loori

Bringing the Sacred to Life: The Daily Practice of Zen Ritual

A home-dwellers Zen liturgy minibook by John Daido Loori. This volume contains chants, dedications, and four chapters to help you make liturgy a vital part of your life at home, at work, or wherever you may find yourself. It shows how we can create liturgy and how we recognize and create sacredness.

Cave of Tigers: The Living Zen Practice of Dharma Combat

A one-of-a kind record of what genuine Zen training can be within the context of an enlivening teacher-student relationship. Culled from formal public meetings over fifteen years, these transcripts convey the excitement and seriousness of practicing on the sharp edge of our self-exploration, with all of its associated rawness, vulnerability, spontaneity, and wonder. The book shows that Zen is alive and well here in America at the turn of the millennium, that it is accessible to all of us, and that it is completely relevant to the ways we live our lives. It is an invitation and a map to exuberant sanity.

Finding the Still Point: A Beginner's Guide to Zen Meditation

Beginner's instruction in zazen, seated Zen meditation—accompanied by an audio CD that includes a short talk on zazen and two timed meditation periods. This book is beautifully and helpfully illustrated.

Hearing with the Eye: Photographs from Point Lobos

John Daido Loori's stunning array of images taken at Point Lobos, California, beautifully complements his commentary on Master Dogen's *Teachings of the Earth*, a profound exploration of the mystical reality of the insentient. The words and images presented in this book are an attempt to enter the hidden universe of the insentient and see "things for what else they are." They are an invitation to discover the full spectrum of the teachings of rocks, mountains, rivers, and trees.

Invoking Reality: Moral and Ethical Teachings of Zen

There is a common misconception that to practice Zen is to practice meditation and nothing else. In truth, the practice of meditation goes hand-in-hand with moral conduct. In *Invoking Reality*, John Daido Loori presents and explains the ethical precepts of Zen as essential aspects of Zen training and development. He provides a modern interpretation of the precepts and discusses the ethical significance of these vows as guidelines for living. "Zen is a practice that takes place within the world," he says, "based on moral and ethical teachings that have been handed down from generation to generation."

Making Love with Light: Contemplating Nature with Words and Photographs

Brings together Loori's talents as an award-winning photographer and Zen teacher. The essays, images, and poems on these pages fill the gap that separates us from ourselves, and from all that is wild, free, and uncultivated. They are an expression of love using light. Seventy-five full-color plates with accompanying Zen poems form a panoramic vista of and give voice to the mountains, rivers, rock, and sky.

Mountain Record of Zen Talks

Explores Zen practice as a spiritual journey of self-discovery: beginning with the development of a sound appreciation of zazen, realizing the ground of being and the nature of reality, and actualizing these insights in the activities of the world.

Teachings of the Earth: Zen and the Environment

How does Zen practice inform our appreciation of our place in the environment? This book shows us that within stillness is a seed of sanity and a gate to hear the teachings and to heal ourselves. A unique exposition of the awakened ecological consciousness implicit in Zen Buddhism.

Printed in the United States
by Baker & Taylor Publisher Services